LET'S TALK LEGACY

Also by Monika Halan

*Let's Talk Money: You've Worked Hard for It,
Now Make It Work for You* (2018)

*Let's Talk Mutual Funds: A Systematic,
Smart Way to Make Them Work for You* (2023)

LET'S TALK LEGACY

A FINANCIAL PLANNER FOR YOUR LOVED ONES

MONIKA HALAN

HARPER BUSINESS

An Imprint of HarperCollins *Publishers*

First published in India by Harper Business 2024
An imprint of HarperCollins *Publishers*
4th Floor, Tower A, Building No. 10, DLF Cyber City,
DLF Phase II, Gurugram, Haryana – 122002
www.harpercollins.co.in

2 4 6 8 10 9 7 5 3 1

Copyright © Monika Halan 2024

P-ISBN: 978-93-6213-999-3
E-ISBN: 978-93-6213-731-9

The views and opinions expressed in this book are the author's own and the facts are as reported by her, and the publishers are not in any way liable for the same.

None of the content in this book is intended to be a substitute for professional financial advice and should not be relied on as financial advice. Always seek the guidance of your financial advisor with any questions you may have regarding your finances.

Monika Halan asserts the moral right
to be identified as the author of this work.

All rights reserved. No part of this publication may be reproduced, stored in a retrieval system, or transmitted, in any form or by any means, electronic, mechanical, photocopying, recording or otherwise, without the prior permission of the publishers.

Typeset in 11/14 Adobe Garamond at
Manipal Technologies Limited, Manipal

Printed and bound at
Thomson Press (India) Ltd

To the families of those whose money sits unclaimed with the government—it just takes a notebook that has the details.

Contents

	Preface	ix
	Introduction	xiii
1.	Basic Documents	1
2.	Banks and Cards	24
3.	Insurance Policies	44
4.	Fixed-Return Investments	66
5.	Capital Markets	82
6.	Real Estate	100
7.	Jewellery, Vehicles and Others (Like Art and Collectibles)	106
8.	Loans	116
9.	Tax	123
10.	Wills	126
	Author's Note	135
	Acknowledgements	137

Preface

I did not plan to die.
 Not yet.

In fact, now that I look back, I did not plan for death at all.

Despite knowing that we all will die someday, I really did think *that* someday was never really going to come. Even when I lit the funeral pyre of my 78-year-old father a few years back, I never stopped to think of my own mortality. Even when my friend had a sudden stroke and died at 45, I worried for a few days about death and then got on with life—bills, office politics, fights with that Mr Awasthi downstairs who blocks the passage with his plants, vacations, the unfinished woodwork in the study and a million things that need my attention.

But then, here I am—dead.

Who'd have thought that a peanut gone the wrong way could snuff out my life at 48—I mean 48! Nobody dies at 48. And here I am—dead. Well, I must be—for I see my body lying there fully dressed in white with flowers and stuff, like you see in the movies, and I see my wife and kids sobbing uncontrollably—I want to reach out and tell them that I am fine—but, I am dead, and I realize that I can't.

It's too late.

And then it hits me—I can't communicate with them at all. Not on a call. Not over a message. Not even a whisper in the ear.

A week later, I see them grappling with the mess I have left behind in my finances. I never involved my wife or kids in any the money decisions or paperwork—it's a man's job, right? And here is my wife, rummaging through my desk, trying to get some numbers from my phone, struggling with my laptop trying to piece together our financial lives.

I wish I could tell them where the insurance policy is. The name and number of the agent. The details of the properties I had bought, where the papers are. The loans I had taken, the stocks and funds I owned. I wish I had recorded all the information so that at least the material part of life could continue without me.

'Hey', exclaimed my wife. 'Wake up! Why are you groaning in your sleep? What's going on? Did you drink too much last night?'

Huh? I wake up with a sudden rush of relief. Those few moments of panic last evening with the peanut stuck briefly in my windpipe must have triggered this nightmare. The morning looks so good. My wife and kids' usual noisy arguments are music. I must tell Mr Awasthi that I actually enjoy his greens.

And before this week is out, I am sitting down and filling the *Let's Talk Legacy* workbook. It is one way—an important way—I express my love for my family. Death is inevitable and, like markets, you can't predict it. Best to leave my family with memories and not a wild goose chase to assets and money that I did not record somewhere.

Enough said: love is keeping, maintaining and sharing financial records. I am filling this book.

May we live long, but just in case we don't, this book will keep my family on course.

Introduction

A friend once told me a story about when he began putting down all his financial details in one place and got his wife to understand them: He was on a flight. The turbulence shook the aircraft and his belief that he was immortal. He pulled out his phone and began tapping out all the details of the financials that his wife might need if this metal bird went down. The people you think of in your last moments are the people you need to protect when you are not in your last moments.

In Chapter 5 of *Let's Talk Money*, I ask you to do this thought experiment. Shut your eyes and imagine you are gone. And then see the family's distress in trying to piece your financial life together. You can't message them from the other side or whisper passwords in their ear as they try and open your mobile and email to access crucial money details.

Specially after Covid, the threat of an untimely death comes very close to all of us. I recommend filling this *Let's Talk Legacy* workbook to help your family get control of the household's finances. The name is self-explanatory. It contains all the relevant information for those left behind. The emotional trauma is incalculable, but a financial hand of support will prevent a further escalation of the disaster that is death.

As you do this exercise, you will realize how useful it is to put all the important financial details in one place and share them with your spouse. The elderly can use this to inform their heirs as to the assets and the mix of distribution.

Although the name of this document and the exercise might sound scary, it comes from the deepest point of love and care. I hope you understand this and look after your loved ones even after you are gone.

How to Use This Book

When I took on what is seen as mainly being a man's job of creating and maintaining assets for the family, I found myself extending the task to record-keeping. I think it is a woman thing to meticulously plan and think for the family's welfare. I encourage even those women, who today might not be a participant in asset-creation, to take over the job of filling this book. It will not only get you familiar with the asset list, you will also know what is in your name.

For me, along with asset-creation came the thought *what if*. What if I am not around? So began the record-keeping.

I must share with you that for years, I have maintained a spiral diary that I use to record all these details. It began with just recording some bank details. But I found myself adding pages each year and putting in more and more information.

I cannot begin to tell you how many times I refer to this book for routine paperwork, retrieving a password that I have forgotten, or getting the bank login and password that has slipped my mind.

Years of doing this has made me a fan of using a pencil for some entries. In fact, my advice is to use a pencil rather than a pen when you start using this book. Some numbers like Aadhaar are fixed, so once you have double-checked the accuracy of the details, you can go ahead and make it permanent.

But there are other details such as passwords that will surely change once in a while. Use a pencil to record these so you can keep adding the new ones.

I know that you are advised to not write your passwords down, but given the number of online relationships we have, there are at least twenty to twenty-five usernames and passwords that we use, and it is impossible to remember each of them. Also, a few people use password-generators instead of making their own. In this case, practicality trumps theoretical advice. Write the passwords down here and then keep this book under lock and key.

You will have to build the habit of opening this book and updating the details as soon as you have made the change.

Feel free to modify pages and add information you think is needed in order to customize the diary to your unique situation.

And last, do not forget to tell your significant other or close family members about this book and its location. Needless to say, keep it safely at all times because this has the life blood of your financial life.

Some people like to create a digital record of these details, but I have two issues with this. One, data can get hacked and you are at the risk of losing your entire secret data to the dark web. Two, if one password is lost or not communicated, the entire repository of details is lost to your family.

A physical book has its own issues of security, but you can choose to keep it locked and inform your spouse or family about the location of the book and the way to access it.

My best wishes to you as you embark on this very empowering journey for your and your family's future.

1
Basic Documents

How often do you scramble to find the documents that are needed for some paperwork or for another round of the unending know-your-customer process at banks? Intersect with a government agency and the desire for documents just rises exponentially. I find that putting down the details of the essential documents for the family all in one place very useful. Specially for the person who does all the paperwork, easy access to the correct documents, numbers and details saves times and increases efficiency. While this is the current use of all these details, the aim of putting these down is to help the family in your absence.

I encourage you to use the following format but feel free to add details that you think are relevant. There are also enough blank spaces left for you to add any document that pertains to your particular situation. There could be club memberships or some other document that is relevant to you and not covered here. There are enough spaces for you to add family members.

Remember that there are some details that are permanent, for example the Aadhaar number, and there are others that could change, for example, the name of the financial planner or lawyer. Fill in the workbook with this in mind—it will help you in the future.

Some organizations ask you to change your password every three months and others allow you to keep using the same password. In any case, it is a good safety protocol to change passwords once in a while. Write them in pencil here.

Filling in the location of the documents is important because the family might not know your filing system or have access to the locker that you might be using. Think this part through. Once a friend's wife almost threw away the paper that had his password thinking it was a scrap! She did not know that he keeps all his documents in a Word file and password-protects it. That password is kept in his office locker. And she almost threw away the password!

In this workbook, you will see a page for benefit cards. This is for those who have special services such as CGHS, or for a defence services benefit card.

When you imagined being an adult and living your own life, who knew the mountain of paperwork that waited as you turned the page on childhood.

Aadhaar

Name	Number
Location of Aadhaar cards	

PAN

Name	Number
Location of PAN cards	

Passport 1

Name	
Number	
Date of issue	
Date of expiry	
Issued at	
Location of passport	

Passport 2

Name	
Number	
Date of issue	
Date of expiry	
Issued at	
Location of passport	

Passport 3

Name	
Number	
Date of issue	
Date of expiry	
Issued at	
Location of passport	

Passport 4

Name	
Number	
Date of issue	
Date of expiry	
Issued at	
Location of passport	

Birth Certificate

Name	Location of certificate

Marriage Certificate

Name	Location of certificate

Driving Licence 1

Name	
Number	
Date of issue	
Date of expiry	
Location of licence	

Driving Licence 2

Name	
Number	
Date of issue	
Date of expiry	
Location of licence	

Voter Card

Name	Number

Location of voter cards

Professional Identifier

(for example, employee code or professional registration number)

Description	
Number	
Details	
Location	

Financial Advisor

Name	
Details	
Email	
Phone	
Address	

Lawyer

Name	
Details	
Email	
Phone	
Address	

Chartered Accountant

Name	
Details	
Email	
Phone	
Address	

Insurance Agent

Name	
Details	
Email	
Phone	
Address	

Stock Broker

Name	
Details	
Email	
Phone	
Address	

Mutual Fund Distributor

Name	
Details	
Email	
Phone	
Address	

Doctor 1

Name	
Speciality	
Email	
Phone	
Address	

Doctor 2

Name	
Speciality	
Email	
Phone	
Address	

Doctor 3

Name	
Speciality	
Email	
Phone	
Address	

Doctor 4

Name	
Speciality	
Email	
Phone	
Address	

Electricity

Service provider	
Helpline number	
Meter number	
Customer ID	
Login details	

Water

Service provider	
Helpline number	
Meter number	
Customer ID	
Login details	

Gas

Service provider	
Helpline number	
Meter number	
Customer ID	
Login details	

Telecom Provider

Service provider	
Helpline number	
Customer ID	
Wi-Fi name	
Wi-Fi password	

OTT Platform 1

Name of platform	
Username	
Password	
Date of subscription start	
Date of renewal	

OTT Platform 2

Name of platform	
Username	
Password	
Date of subscription start	
Date of renewal	

OTT Platform 3

Name of platform	
Username	
Password	
Date of subscription start	
Date of renewal	

OTT Platform 4

Name of platform	
Username	
Password	
Date of subscription start	
Date of renewal	

Email and Social Media

Email	
Password	
Email	
Password	
Email	
Password	

X

Username	
Password	

Instagram

Username	
Password	

LinkedIn	
Username	
Password	
Facebook	
Username	
Password	
Others	
Username	
Password	
Username	
Password	
Username	
Password	

Benefit Card 1

Issuing authority	
Card number	
Issue date	
Expiry date	
Location of card	

Benefit Card 2

Issuing authority	
Card number	
Issue date	
Expiry date	
Location of card	

Club Membership 1

Issuing agency	
Card number	
Issue date	
Expiry date	
Location of card	

Club Membership 2

Issuing agency	
Card number	
Issue date	
Expiry date	
Location of card	

Will 1

Name	
Date of will	
Location of will	
Executor name	
Executor contact details	
Witness 1 name	
Witness 1 contact details	
Witness 2 name	
Witness 2 contact details	

Will 2

Name	
Date of will	
Location of will	
Executor name	
Executor contact details	
Witness 1 name	
Witness 1 contact details	
Witness 2 name	
Witness 2 contact details	

2
Banks and Cards

Did you know that in India, unclaimed bank deposits were over Rs 35,000 crore as at the end of February 2023? Many people open bank accounts and forget to tell their family, and worse, don't put nominee details for the accounts. The pages in this chapter are aimed at helping you record details of every bank account, every card you own and all the relevant information pertaining to each account.

There is space for more than one bank account because over the course of life, people end up with several of them. Each time a job is changed, a new salary account gets opened. Then there are the legacy accounts from childhood or joint accounts with the spouse. Having a line of sight on each bank account and its basic details is useful, else there is the scramble to get the IFSC code of a bank for some paperwork, or the branch address is needed for some purpose. Not only do you need these details handy, you also need to know the location of the cheque book and pass books (for those who still use them).

As you fill these sheets, keep in mind the importance of filling nominee details. It is also an alert to check with your bank if your nominations are in place. For the family that gets to use this document, it is useful to know who the nominee is and how to apportion the funds in the various bank accounts.

I hope you are using the three-bank account system I have described in *Let's Talk Money* to create an Income account, a Spend It account and an Invest It account. Write against the bank name the purpose of that account. It helps to earmark each bank to a specific purpose such as spending or collecting savings.

If you record your account as a 'joint', use the extra space to put down what type of a joint account it is, for example, you might write 'either or survivor'. Check your bank documents to see the type of account you have.

Most people will have a Resident Indian (RI) bank account, but you, or your family, could have NRO or NRE accounts. If you want to add more information, such as a SWIFT code, you can write it in the same space as the IFSC code—there is enough space there.

Again, be careful to use a pencil when filling in the passwords for your internet banking—these could keep changing. If you are using a pin number for your banking app, use the internet banking space to record it as well. Again, use a pencil as you might want to change the pin number.

Bank 1

Name	
Saving or current	
Single or joint	
First holder	
Second holder	
Nominee	
Type of account	RI ☐ NRO ☐ NRE ☐ Other ☐
Branch address	
Account number	
IFSC Code	
Location of cheque book	
Internet banking	
Username	
Password	
PIN	

Bank 2

Name	
Saving or current	
Single or joint	
First holder	
Second holder	
Nominee	
Type of account	RI ☐ NRO ☐ NRE ☐ Other ☐
Branch address	
Account number	
IFSC Code	
Location of cheque book	
Internet banking	
Username	
Password	
PIN	

Bank 3

Name	
Saving or current	
Single or joint	
First holder	
Second holder	
Nominee	
Type of account	RI ☐ NRO ☐ NRE ☐ Other ☐
Branch address	
Account number	
IFSC Code	
Location of cheque book	
Internet banking	
Username	
Password	
PIN	

Bank 4

Name	
Saving or current	
Single or joint	
First holder	
Second holder	
Nominee	
Type of account	RI ☐ NRO ☐ NRE ☐ Other ☐
Branch address	
Account number	
IFSC Code	
Location of cheque book	
Internet banking	
Username	
Password	
PIN	

Fixed Deposit 1

Bank name	
FD number	
Joint or single	
First holder	
Second holder	
Date and amount of deposit	
Date and amount at maturity	
Location of FD certificate	
Name of nominee	
Relationship	

Fixed Deposit 2

Bank name	
FD number	
Joint or single	
First holder	
Second holder	
Date and amount of deposit	
Date and amount at maturity	
Location of FD certificate	
Name of nominee	
Relationship	

Fixed Deposit 3

Bank name	
FD number	
Joint or single	
First holder	
Second holder	
Date and amount of deposit	
Date and amount at maturity	
Location of FD certificate	
Name of nominee	
Relationship	

Fixed Deposit 4

Bank name	
FD number	
Joint or single	
First holder	
Second holder	
Date and amount of deposit	
Date and amount at maturity	
Location of FD certificate	
Name of nominee	
Relationship	

Locker 1

Bank name	
Branch	
Locker number	
Key number	
Location of key	
Single or joint	
First holder	
Second holder	
Name of nominee	
Relationship	
Contents of locker	

Locker 2

Bank name	
Branch	
Locker number	
Key number	
Location of key	
Single or joint	
First holder	
Second holder	
Name of nominee	
Relationship	
Contents of locker	

Credit Card 1

Name of bank	
Visa/Mastercard/Others	
Name on card	
Card number	
CVV	
Date of issue	
Date of expiry	
PIN	
Location	
Any insurance benefits	
Helpline number	
Online access details	

Credit Card 2

Name of bank	
Visa/Mastercard/Others	
Name on card	
Card number	
CVV	
Date of issue	
Date of expiry	
PIN	
Location	
Any insurance benefits	
Helpline number	
Online access details	

Credit Card 3

Name of bank	
Visa/Mastercard/Others	
Name on card	
Card number	
CVV	
Date of issue	
Date of expiry	
PIN	
Location	
Any insurance benefits	
Helpline number	
Online access details	

Credit Card 4

Name of bank	
Visa/Mastercard/Others	
Name on card	
Card number	
CVV	
Date of issue	
Date of expiry	
PIN	
Location	
Any insurance benefits	
Helpline number	
Online access details	

Debit Card 1

Name of bank	
Visa/Mastercard/Others	
Name on card	
Card number	
CVV	
Date of issue	
Date of expiry	
PIN	
Location	
Any insurance benefits	
Helpline number	
Online access details	

Debit Card 2

Name of bank	
Visa/Mastercard/Others	
Name on card	
Card number	
CVV	
Date of issue	
Date of expiry	
PIN	
Location	
Any insurance benefits	
Helpline number	
Online access details	

Debit Card 3

Name of bank	
Visa/Mastercard/Others	
Name on card	
Card number	
CVV	
Date of issue	
Date of expiry	
PIN	
Location	
Any insurance benefits	
Helpline number	
Online access details	

Debit Card 4

Name of bank	
Visa/Mastercard/Others	
Name on card	
Card number	
CVV	
Date of issue	
Date of expiry	
PIN	
Location	
Any insurance benefits	
Helpline number	
Online access details	

3

Insurance Policies

Insurance is bought to mitigate future emergencies, such as an untimely death, an accident or a vehicle theft. When an emergency hits, most homes see a scramble for documents, such as those needed for hospitalization and then for the claim. It is important to put down details of the various policies that are bought in one place to get a clean line of sight on what covers are available and where the documents might be.

I am sure you know that the unclaimed money with Indian life insurance companies runs into tens of crores of rupees—the IRDAI annual report puts the number at more than Rs 200 crore unclaimed for the year 2022–23. People buy policies and omit to tell their families about it. Buying a policy is not enough, there is the work to maintain it and have the details ready for your family in case you are not around to help with essential information. My advice is to fill these sheets carefully as the claim might depend on the accuracy of information, and the help that you can give through simple documentation is really worth the work put in today.

As you fill these sheets, go back and read the chapters on insurance in *Let's Talk Money* again to review your own policies. Remember that a life cover is best bought through a pure term life cover and not through bundled insurance plans.

I have left a number of pages for life insurance—although you only need that one term plan—because most people end up being sold multiple policies over the years.

Insurance policies are sold by a variety of distribution channels: it is important for you to fill the details of the agent or agency that sold you the policy. The fat commission you pay agents entitles you to get service right till the end of the policy. In the event of a claim, you need the agent to help with the paperwork and claim process. So, record these details carefully. If you have bought a policy online, then use the space left for the agent and details to record your online username and password.

In the space for health insurance, you must fill in the Third Party Administrator (TPA) details. The TPAs help to connect you, the hospital and the insurance company, and are a key part of the claims process.

Life Insurance 1

Name of life insurance company	
Name of the insured	
Name of policy	
Policy number	
Date of issue	
Date of maturity	
Date of premium payment	
Premium paying term	
Sum assured	
Name of agent	
Contact details of agent	
Location of policy document	
Names of beneficiaries, relationship	
Benefit stream for investment-oriented insurance plans	

Life Insurance 2

Name of life insurance company	
Name of the insured	
Name of policy	
Policy number	
Date of issue	
Date of maturity	
Date of premium payment	
Premium paying term	
Sum assured	
Name of agent	
Contact details of agent	
Location of policy document	
Names of beneficiaries, relationship	
Benefit stream for investment-oriented insurance plans	

Life Insurance 3

Name of life insurance company	
Name of the insured	
Name of policy	
Policy number	
Date of issue	
Date of maturity	
Date of premium payment	
Premium paying term	
Sum assured	
Name of agent	
Contact details of agent	
Location of policy document	
Names of beneficiaries, relationship	
Benefit stream for investment-oriented insurance plans	

Life Insurance 4

Name of life insurance company	
Name of the insured	
Name of policy	
Policy number	
Date of issue	
Date of maturity	
Date of premium payment	
Premium paying term	
Sum assured	
Name of agent	
Contact details of agent	
Location of policy document	
Names of beneficiaries, relationship	
Benefit stream for investment-oriented insurance plans	

Life Insurance 5

Name of life insurance company	
Name of the insured	
Name of policy	
Policy number	
Date of issue	
Date of maturity	
Date of premium payment	
Premium paying term	
Sum assured	
Name of agent	
Contact details of agent	
Location of policy document	
Names of beneficiaries, relationship	
Benefit stream for investment-oriented insurance plans	

Life Insurance 6

Name of life insurance company	
Name of the insured	
Name of policy	
Policy number	
Date of issue	
Date of maturity	
Date of premium payment	
Premium paying term	
Sum assured	
Name of agent	
Contact details of agent	
Location of policy document	
Names of beneficiaries, relationship	
Benefit stream for investment-oriented insurance plans	

Health Insurance 1

Name of health insurance company	
Name of policy	
Persons covered	
Policy number	
Date of issue	
Date of premium payment	
Sum insured	
Location of mediclaim card	
Location of policy document	
TPA name	
TPA number	
Agent name	
Agent number	
Names of nominees	
Relationship	

Health Insurance 2

Name of health insurance company	
Name of policy	
Persons covered	
Policy number	
Date of issue	
Date of premium payment	
Sum insured	
Location of mediclaim card	
Location of policy document	
TPA name	
TPA number	
Agent name	
Agent number	
Names of nominees	
Relationship	

CGHS or Other Benefits 1

Name of holder	
Document number	
Names of beneficiaries	
Relationship	
Validity	
Location of cards	

CGHS or Other Benefits 2

Name of holder	
Document number	
Names of beneficiaries	
Relationship	
Validity	
Location of cards	

CGHS or Other Benefits 3

Name of holder	
Document number	
Names of beneficiaries	
Relationship	
Validity	
Location of cards	

CGHS or Other Benefits 4

Name of holder	
Document number	
Names of beneficiaries	
Relationship	
Validity	
Location of cards	

Vehicle Insurance 1

Vehicle owner name	
Vehicle insured	
Insurance company name	
Name of policy	
Policy number	
Date of issue	
Date of premium payment	
Sum insured	
Location of policy document	
Agent name and number	
Names of nominees	
Relationship	
Details of cover	

Vehicle Insurance 2

Vehicle owner name	
Vehicle insured	
Insurance company name	
Name of policy	
Policy number	
Date of issue	
Date of premium payment	
Sum insured	
Location of policy document	
Agent name and number	
Names of nominees	
Relationship	
Details of cover	

Vehicle Insurance 3

Vehicle owner name	
Vehicle insured	
Insurance company name	
Name of policy	
Policy number	
Date of issue	
Date of premium payment	
Sum insured	
Location of policy document	
Agent name and number	
Names of nominees	
Relationship	
Details of cover	

Vehicle Insurance 4

Vehicle owner name	
Vehicle insured	
Insurance company name	
Name of policy	
Policy number	
Date of issue	
Date of premium payment	
Sum insured	
Location of policy document	
Agent name and number	
Names of nominees	
Relationship	
Details of cover	

Home Insurance 1

Name of holder	
Address of home covered	
Name of policy	
Policy number	
Date of issue	
Date of premium payment	
Sum insured	
Location of policy document	
Agent name and number	
Names of nominees	
Relationship	
Details of cover	

Home Insurance 2

Name of holder	
Address of home covered	
Name of policy	
Policy number	
Date of issue	
Date of premium payment	
Sum insured	
Location of policy document	
Agent name and number	
Names of nominees	
Relationship	
Details of cover	

Group and Corporate Cover 1

Company that gives the group cover	
Name of insurance company	
Name of holder	
Name of policy	
Policy number	
Date of issue	
Date of premium payment if any	
Sum insured	
Location of policy document	
Agent/accounts name and number	
Names of nominees	
Relationship	
Details of cover	

Group and Corporate Cover 2

Company that gives the group cover	
Name of insurance company	
Name of holder	
Name of policy	
Policy number	
Date of issue	
Date of premium payment if any	
Sum insured	
Location of policy document	
Agent/accounts name and number	
Names of nominees	
Relationship	
Details of cover	

Other Policies 1

Name of holder	
Name of insurance company	
Name of policy	
Policy number	
Date of issue	
Date of premium payment	
Sum insured	
Location of policy document	
Agent/account name and number	
Names of nominees	
Relationship	
Details of cover	

Other Policies 2

Name of holder	
Name of insurance company	
Name of policy	
Policy number	
Date of issue	
Date of premium payment	
Sum insured	
Location of policy document	
Agent/account name and number	
Names of nominees	
Relationship	
Details of cover	

4

Fixed-Return Investments

Products included in this chapter sit in the fixed-return category of assets, other than fixed deposits. They have fixed or guaranteed returns, including the small savings products and various government schemes. The list here is not exhaustive since products keep getting added or removed by the government. I have left enough 'other products' pages for you to fill in the details of products not covered.

As you fill these sheets, remember to update changes in balances, passwords and product details as they take place. Doing an annual audit is a good idea to see the products you have and what the current value is. It will also help to build your net worth statement by adding up the assets from these sheets. I have left four sheets for the Employees' Provident Fund (EPF) accounts. You can use this in three ways. One, for those who change jobs often and want to record the details of their provident fund from each organization. Of course, in the back end, the PF is now connected to a number that is carried forward company to company. Two, for those who want to record the PF details of other family members. Three, for those retired, who want to record their pension streams—use the EPF pages to fill your pension details.

I have left two pages for Public Provident Fund (PPF) for those whose spouse too has the account, and they would like to record it here. There is space to record the PPF assets for every year that you complete. Do remember to write the interest rates for each year just so that you know what rate you got over the life of the product.

Many of you might be using online access to several of these products and might not have a physical certificate. Use that box to record any other important detail that you think you'd need and I have not included.

Some products have interest rates that keep changing over the life of the investment. There is enough white space left on the page for you to record this in the margins.

Employees' Provident Fund 1

Name of holder	
Universal Account Number	
UAN card location	
Scheme certificate number	
Name of employer	
Date of joining	
Online access details	
Names of nominees	
Relationship	
PF balance	

Employees' Provident Fund 2

Name of holder	
Universal Account Number	
UAN card location	
Scheme certificate number	
Name of employer	
Date of joining	
Online access details	
Names of nominees	
Relationship	
PF balance	

Employees' Provident Fund 3

Name of holder	
Universal Account Number	
UAN card location	
Scheme certificate number	
Name of employer	
Date of joining	
Online access details	
Names of nominees	
Relationship	
PF balance	

Employees' Provident Fund 4

Name of holder	
Universal Account Number	
UAN card location	
Scheme certificate number	
Name of employer	
Date of joining	
Online access details	
Names of nominees	
Relationship	
PF balance	

Public Provident Fund 1

Bank/post office name and address	
Start year	
End year	
Names of nominees	
Relationship	

Assets in each financial year

Year 1	Year 2
Year 3	Year 4
Year 5	Year 6
Year 7	Year 8
Year 9	Year 10
Year 11	Year 12
Year 13	Year 14
Year 15	Year 16

Public Provident Fund 2

Bank/post office name and address	
Start year	
End year	
Names of nominees	
Relationship	

Assets in each financial year	
Year 1	Year 2
Year 3	Year 4
Year 5	Year 6
Year 7	Year 8
Year 9	Year 10
Year 11	Year 12
Year 13	Year 14
Year 15	Year 16

National Savings Certificate 1

Bank/PO bought from	
NSC number	
Date of purchase	
Date of maturity	
Interest rate	
Names of nominees, relationship	

National Savings Certificate 2

Bank/PO bought from	
NSC number	
Date of purchase	
Date of maturity	
Interest rate	
Names of nominees, relationship	

Post Office Monthly Income Scheme 1

Bank/PO bought from	
Certificate number	
Amount invested	
Monthly income and interest	
Date of purchase	
Date of maturity	
Location of certificate	
Names of nominees, relationship	

Post Office Monthly Income Scheme 2

Bank/PO bought from	
Certificate number	
Amount invested	
Monthly income and interest	
Date of purchase	
Date of maturity	
Location of certificate	
Names of nominees, relationship	

Recurring Deposit 1

Bank/PO bought from	
Certificate number	
Amount invested per month	
Date of purchase and interest	
Date and amount at maturity	
Location of certificate	
Names of nominees, relationship	

Recurring Deposit 2

Bank/PO bought from	
Certificate number	
Amount invested per month	
Date of purchase and interest	
Date and amount at maturity	
Location of certificate	
Names of nominees, relationship	

Kisan Vikas Patra 1

Bank/PO bought from	
Certificate number	
Amount invested	
Date of purchase and interest	
Date and amount at maturity	
Location of certificate	
Names of nominees, relationship	

Kisan Vikas Patra 2

Bank/PO bought from	
Certificate number	
Amount invested	
Date of purchase and interest	
Date and amount at maturity	
Location of certificate	
Names of nominees, relationship	

RBI Bond 1

Bank/vendor bought from	
Bond number	
Amount invested	
Date of purchase and interest	
Date and amount at maturity	
Names of nominees, relationship	

RBI Bond 2

Bank/vendor bought from	
Bond number	
Amount invested	
Date of purchase and interest	
Date and amount at maturity	
Names of nominees, relationship	

Company Deposits 1

Company	
Certificate number	
Amount invested	
Date of purchase and interest	
Date and amount at maturity	
Names of nominees, relationship	

Company Deposits 2

Company	
Certificate number	
Amount invested	
Date of purchase and interest	
Date and amount at maturity	
Names of nominees, relationship	

Others 1

Bank/vendor bought from	
Certificate number	
Amount invested	
Date of purchase and interest	
Date and amount at maturity	
Names of nominees, relationship	

Others 2

Bank/vendor bought from	
Certificate number	
Amount invested	
Date of purchase and interest	
Date and amount at maturity	
Names of nominees, relationship	

Others 3

Bank/vendor bought from	
Certificate number	
Amount invested	
Date of purchase and interest	
Date and amount at maturity	
Names of nominees, relationship	

Others 4

Bank/vendor bought from	
Certificate number	
Amount invested	
Date of purchase and interest	
Date and amount at maturity	
Names of nominees, relationship	

5

Capital Markets

Unlike earlier, capital market products such as stocks, mutual funds and other listed securities now form a growing part of the asset allocation of Indians. One estimate says that over 17 per cent of all Indian households have at least some holding in the stock market either directly or through an intermediary such as in a mutual fund. In fact, if we add the share of EPFO's investments in the stock market and the share of NPS, the number could be much higher.

The pages in this chapter are meant for you to write down the capital market relationships, rather than map the daily changes in the portfolio values. Given that there are various ways to buy and sell capital market products and you must write down the relevant details that your survivors will need to access the funds. As you fill, you will also remember to update your nominee details with your service providers.

The value of your portfolio will change every day and there is no point in recording the names of stocks or mutual fund schemes here. The latest details are available in the account statements and broker accounts. Therefore, put down the details of the intermediaries through whom you buy and sell these products. Many people now invest directly online or through apps. It is a good idea to record your method of accessing markets here along with the details needed to use the account.

The boxes in the 'portfolio value' pages are large enough for you to record the capital gains or losses realized in each year. Just for your own knowledge, write down the year-ending Sensex or Nifty50 value, or that of any other benchmark that you use, to see how the markets have done over the years.

The National Pension System (NPS) has emerged as a viable option to target a retirement corpus. Many of you use the Tier II accounts along with the long-term Tier I product, so don't forget to add those details here. One part of the NPS page will only get filled when you reach retirement age and choose your annuity provider.

There are new products coming to the market every day. The pages given for PMS and others are aimed at allowing you to record these. If this space changes drastically, look out for future editions of this book!

Stock Market 1

Name of holder	
Depository name	
Depository participant name	
Depository participant ID	
Client ID	
Consolidated account statement location	
Broker name	
Broker website	
Username	
Password	
Relationship manager name	
Contact details	
Names of nominees, relationship	

Portfolio Value	
Date	Amount

Stock Market 2

Name of holder	
Depository name	
Depository participant name	
Depository participant ID	
Client ID	
Consolidated account statement location	
Broker name	
Broker website	
Username	
Password	
Relationship manager name	
Contact details	
Names of nominees, relationship	

Portfolio Value	
Date	Amount

Mutual Funds 1

Name of holder	
Name of bank/platform/ agent/advisor	
Client ID	
Consolidated account statement location	
Website	
Username	
Password	
Relationship manager name	
Contact details	
Names of nominees, relationship	

Portfolio Value	
Date	Amount

Mutual Funds 2

Name of holder	
Name of bank/platform/agent/advisor	
Client ID	
Consolidated account statement location	
Website	
Username	
Password	
Relationship manager name	
Contact details	
Names of nominees, relationship	

Portfolio Value	
Date	Amount

National Pension System 1

Name of holder	
PRAN	
Registration date	
Tier I details	
Tier II details	
Point of Presence service provider	
Online access details	
Annuity service provider	
Transaction statement location	
Names of nominees, relationship	

Portfolio Value	
Date	Amount

National Pension System 2

Name of holder	
PRAN	
Registration date	
Tier I details	
Tier II details	
Point of Presence service provider	
Online access details	
Annuity service provider	
Transaction statement location	
Names of nominees, relationship	

Portfolio Value	
Date	Amount

PMS, AIFs, REITs and Others 1

Name of product	
Name of holder	
Client ID	
Name of bank/platform/agent/advisor	
Website	
Username	
Password	
Relationship manager name	
Contact details	
Transaction statement location	
Names of nominees, relationship	

Portfolio Value	
Date	Amount

PMS, AIFs, REITs and Others 2

Name of product	
Name of holder	
Client ID	
Name of bank/platform/agent/advisor	
Website	
Username	
Password	
Relationship manager name	
Contact details	
Transaction statement location	
Names of nominees, relationship	

Portfolio Value	
Date	Amount

6

Real Estate

Indians love their property investments, and some people end up with multiple assets over various cities. While managing them remains a difficult task, the mess that is left behind for the heirs to sort out on the death of the property owner is even more challenging. And did you know that real estate is the core of family disputes over generations. One estimate says that more than half the cases pending in Indian courts relate to property disputes.

By filling these sheets, I hope that you will also give your heirs a line of sight on what share of the property or which property they stand to inherit. Therefore, it helps to have all the needed details together in one place at a glance—not just for your heirs but even for you as you begin to build your net worth statement.

I am leaving four sheets for property, actually hoping that you don't fill more than one! Real estate is a difficult asset to maintain and transact in. Worse, I find that it is a clunky asset to inherit with much paperwork and running around needed. As you fill these sheets, keep in mind to add any other relevant detail that is particular to you. It is a good idea to also update your will as you write down the property details below and indicate clearly who gets which property or in what share in case of your demise.

Many people with multiple properties rent them out for income. It is important to record the details of the tenants here. Tenants can keep changing, so remember to use a pencil to record details that are liable to change.

For your own reference, you can add in the margins the value of the property when you bought it and what it is valued periodically. You can also keep adding the periodic spends on maintenance that you might do on the properties. This will come in useful in case you want to sell the property.

For those who have invested the profits of a sale of property in 54EC bonds, add these bonds on the 'others' page.

Property tax is now paid online, so it is a good idea to put down the online access details in the space given for property tax.

Property 1	
Address	
Name of holders	
Share of holders	
Location of papers	
Property identification number	
Details of property	
Mutation details	
Property tax details	
Property on rent/vacant/self-occupied	
Details of tenants	
Name	
Contact details	
Rent per month	

Property 2

Address	
Name of holders	
Share of holders	
Location of papers	
Property identification number	
Details of property	
Mutation details	
Property tax details	
Property on rent/vacant/self-occupied	
Details of tenants	
Name	
Contact details	
Rent per month	

Property 3

Address	
Name of holders	
Share of holders	
Location of papers	
Property identification number	
Details of property	
Mutation details	
Property tax details	
Property on rent/vacant/self-occupied	
Details of tenants	
Name	
Contact details	
Rent per month	

Property 4

Address	
Name of holders	
Share of holders	
Location of papers	
Property identification number	
Details of property	
Mutation details	
Property tax details	
Property on rent/vacant/self-occupied	
Details of tenants	
Name	
Contact details	
Rent per month	

7

Jewellery, Vehicles and Others (Like Art and Collectibles)

Indian households are believed to hold more than 21,000 tonnes of gold, making us the world's largest holders of this shiny metal. Most Indian households have a certain amount of jewellery—both inherited and self-made. But often the gold and jewellery are not properly documented. This becomes important when it is time for an intergenerational transfer of assets.

Therefore, it helps to document this jewellery and get a valuation certificate from an approved valuer. Not only does it give a clear understanding of what is owned, but a valuer report is important for insuring the valuables against theft.

As you fill these pages, remember to update your will as well so that you are able to indicate the inheritors of each piece of jewellery. The value of these assets will continue to change, so you might want to do a periodic update of the value—both for your own understanding and for updating the insurance amounts.

In addition to jewellery, the average middle-class Indian also owns at least one vehicle, if not more. Each time I revisit the locality I grew up in, it is difficult to find parking. These colonies, built in the 1970s, were not planned for people with cars, but for people with cycles and maybe two-wheelers. However, now the roads are choked with cars double-parked in all the lanes, making navigation impossible. The price we pay for emerging affluence!

As a vehicle owner, it is important to document the basic details of each vehicle. Most of these details are available on the registration certificate (RC) and on your insurance policy. I remember filling the online forms for a change in address on the RC and needed all these details at short notice. I remember being thankful for having them at hand in my own record book that I have maintained all these years. You also need to record the details of the person or agency to whom you sell your car. You could also record the FASTag details in the margins of the pages.

In addition to jewellery and vehicles, a household may have some art or some old valuable coins or other collectibles. Some people put a huge value to the silk sarees they own. Others to a collection of pens. The details, value and nomination for each of these assets must be put down in these pages. If you are unable to value, just indicate who that collectible will go to in the event of your passing away.

Jewellery

Location	
Valuation	

Description of jewellery	
Description	Weight

Nominee

Nominee 1	
Name, relationship	
Description of jewellery to be given	
Nominee 2	
Name, relationship	
Description of jewellery to be given	
Nominee 3	
Name, relationship	
Description of jewellery to be given	
Nominee 4	
Name, relationship	
Description of jewellery to be given	

Vehicle 1

Owner name	
Make and model	
Registration number	
Location of RC	
Date of registration	
Registration validity	
Chassis number	
Engine motor number	
Buyer details (if sold)	

Vehicle 2

Owner name	
Make and model	
Registration number	
Location of RC	
Date of registration	
Registration validity	
Chassis number	
Engine motor number	
Buyer details (if sold)	

Vehicle 3

Owner name	
Make and model	
Registration number	
Location of RC	
Date of registration	
Registration validity	
Chassis number	
Engine motor number	
Buyer details (if sold)	

Vehicle 4

Owner name	
Make and model	
Registration number	
Location of RC	
Date of registration	
Registration validity	
Chassis number	
Engine motor number	
Buyer details (if sold)	

Others

Description	Location

Description	Location

8

Loans

Most people are borrowers and lenders, both, in different times of their lives. Loans help to leverage future income and own the asset today rather than build up a corpus to buy it cash down. The use of loans has increased dramatically over the past few years. In fact, in 2023, retail lending grew by 18 per cent and personal loans and credit card spending grew at 22 per cent and 28 per cent, respectively, over the previous year.

Most people begin their debt journey through a vehicle loan and then move onto a larger investment in a house through a home loan. Remember to record the names of all the borrowers and their share of the equated monthly instalments (EMI). This will be useful when you file your tax returns as some loans such as the home loan come along with tax benefits.

You might have a student loan or a personal loan or a loan against property—you must use the pages for 'other loans' to record these. Some people use mobile apps to take loans. It is a good idea to record the loan amount, the interest rate to be paid, the duration of the loan and the EMI to be paid. Even for closed loans, having the details handy for tax purposes is a good idea. Also remember to buy a pure term life insurance policy to cover each loan taken. Some people take a loan on their credit cards or from friends and family.

Record each loan to see the magnitude of the debt you might be in. When you have put down all the loans, their EMIs and the interest rates, do a check on the total EMI you are paying out each month—ideally your total EMIs should be no more than 30 per cent of your take-home income. Also, when you write down all the interest rates that you have to pay, start aggressively paying back the highest interest loans first. Usually a home loan is one of the lowest cost loans because it is a secured loan (secured against the value of the property) and also because of the tax breaks on both principal and interest. This is the last loan you should pay back—target other higher cost loans first.

You might not be a borrower but a lender and have lent money to a family member or a friend. These are the most difficult loans to get repaid, but it is important to keep a record of how much you have lent out as well. Mostly when we lend to family and friends, we don't charge interest; if you happen to do that, do record it in the pages for loans given.

I hope that as time goes by, you never turn to these pages, as you go debt-free—both as a borrower and as a lender.

Home loan 1

Name of lender	
Names of borrowers	
Amount of loan	
Start of EMI	
EMI amount	
Rate of interest	
Date of loan closure	

Home loan 2

Name of lender	
Names of borrowers	
Amount of loan	
Start of EMI	
EMI amount	
Rate of interest	
Date of loan closure	

Vehicle loan 1

Name of lender	
Names of borrowers	
Amount of loan	
Start of EMI	
EMI amount	
Rate of interest	
Date of loan closure	

Vehicle loan 2

Name of lender	
Names of borrowers	
Amount of loan	
Start of EMI	
EMI amount	
Rate of interest	
Date of loan closure	

Other loans 1

Name of lender	
Names of borrowers	
Amount of loan	
Start of EMI	
EMI amount	
Rate of interest	
Date of loan closure	

Other loans 2

Name of lender	
Names of borrowers	
Amount of loan	
Start of EMI	
EMI amount	
Rate of interest	
Date of loan closure	

Other loans 3

Name of lender	
Names of borrowers	
Amount of loan	
Start of EMI	
EMI amount	
Rate of interest	
Date of loan closure	

Other loans 4

Name of lender	
Names of borrowers	
Amount of loan	
Start of EMI	
EMI amount	
Rate of interest	
Date of loan closure	

Loans Given 1

Name of borrower	
Amount lent	
Date lent	
Due date	

Loans Given 2

Name of borrower	
Amount lent	
Date lent	
Due date	

Loans Given 3

Name of borrower	
Amount lent	
Date lent	
Due date	

9
Tax

The annual exercise for the salaried, and the quarterly one for the gig worker and consultant is one that keeps us most on our toes. The fear of a fine or worse keeps most people's tax papers in order. Some people have physical files, others store the papers digitally. Whatever the method, there is already some order in the tax papers that might be missing from the other assets people own.

These pages are meant to complete the picture of your financial life with the tax details in one place. I am leaving two pages for tax for your own use and to add the name of a family member that you file taxes for.

Most people would maintain detailed records on a computer—you can write the file name and the location of that file on the computer in these pages as well. Remember you are creating this for a time that you are not around to tell someone where to look in your computer.

Taxpayer 1

Name of taxpayer	
PAN number	
GST number	
Name of CA	
Contact details of CA	
Username for online tax portal	
Password	
Location of tax related papers	
Details of online tax-related files	

Taxpayer 2

Name of taxpayer	
PAN number	
GST number	
Name of CA	
Contact details of CA	
Username for online tax portal	
Password	
Location of tax-related papers	
Details of online tax-related files	

10
Wills

There is no right age for writing your will. I remember making mine in my thirties, updating it as my minor child became a major and then revising the asset list periodically to reflect the true net worth.

A will is an important document that not only puts down your wishes on how your assets must be disbursed in black and white, but also forces you to do the work needed to consolidate your assets.

For most people who do this, it is the moment of truth of your financial journey when you come face to face with the assets you have, and the work left to do to build for your own future and that of your children.

The work you have done till now in recording your assets will now come in useful. You need to know what you have before you bequeath it.

As you use the will template given on the next few pages, here are some points to note before you begin the process:

- Make individual wills for yourself and your spouse.
- There is no legal requirement for a stamp paper—any paper will do.
- There is no legal requirement to get the will registered, though it is a good idea to do so specially if there is a dispute in the family (or likely to be).
- A will needs an executor—choose one who is younger than you and is a relative or a friend of the family. The executor should not be the beneficiary.
- You need two witnesses for your signature on the will. They don't need to know the contents of the will. You need to record the witnesses' names, dates of birth, addresses, phone numbers, email addresses, and PAN and Aadhaar numbers. The beneficiaries must not be the witnesses.
- You need to initial each page and then sign on the last, and so do the witnesses.

A small warning: Despite the will, most heirs will still have a runaround with lawyers and paperwork to get the assets. But the presence of a will facilitates smoother transfer, especially if there are disputes in the family.

Last Will and Testament of _____ **(FULL NAME)**

I, _____ (FULL NAME), husband/wife of _____ (NAME OF WIFE/HUSBAND), daughter/son of _____ (NAME OF PARENTS), born _____ (DATE OF BIRTH) in _____ (CITY, COUNTRY), resident of _____
_____ (ADDRESS), India, do hereby revoke all my former wills, codicils and testamentary dispositions made by me. I declare this to be my last will and testament.

I maintain good health and possess a sound mind. This will is made by me of my own independent decision and free volition. I have not been influenced, cajoled or coerced in any manner whatsoever.

The name of my husband/wife is _____ (FULL NAME), born _____ (DATE OF BIRTH), in _____ (CITY, COUNTRY). His/her _____ (AADHAAR/PAN/ANY IDENTIFICATION) is _____ (NUMBER).

We have _____ (NUMBER) children, namely:

Child 1 MR/MS FULL NAME, born DOB in CITY, COUNTRY.

___

Child 2 MR/MS FULL NAME, born DOB in CITY, COUNTRY.

___

Child 3 MR/MS FULL NAME, born DOB in CITY, COUNTRY.

___

Child 4 MR/MS FULL NAME, born DOB in CITY, COUNTRY.

___

I own the following immovable and movable assets.

Schedule A: Immoveable assets

Address of the property	Particulars	Size
1.	x/y share	
2.	x/y share	
3.	x/y share	
4.	x/y share	
5.	x/y share	

Schedule B: Moveable assets

Name of the asset	Particulars	Details
Bank accounts		
Lockers		
Financial assets		
Gold, jewellery and cars		

It is advised to attach sheets for schedules A and B.

My PAN number is:

My Aadhaar number is:

I hereby appoint Mr/Ms _____ (NAME), son/daughter of _____ (NAME), resident of _____ _____ (ADDRESS, PHONE, EMAIL) as the executor of this will. His/her Aadhaar number is _____. In the event of Mr/Ms _____'s (NAME) demise, Mr/Ms _____ (NAME), son/daughter of _____ (NAME),

resident of _____
_____ (ADDRESS, PHONE, EMAIL) will be the executor of this will. His/her Aadhaar number is _____.

All the assets owned by me are self-acquired properties and assets. No one else has any right, title, interest, claim or demand whatsoever on these assets or properties. I have full right, absolute power and complete authority on these assets, or on any other property which may be substituted in their place or places, which may be acquired or received by me hereafter.

I hereby give, devise and bequeath all my properties, whether movable or immovable, whatsoever and wheresoever, to my spouse, i.e. _____ (NAME), in the event of my predeceasing him/her. And, subsequently, in the event of his/her demise, my children _____ _____ (NAMES) are the sole heirs in equal* proportion of all the assets I own. In the event where we, both myself and my spouse, are not living any more, I hereby give, devise and bequeath all my properties, whether movable or immovable, to our children _____ (NAMES)

....

* Or whatever you want to give; you can also earmark specific assets for specific people.

in equal[†] proportions. If any or all of the children predecease us, then the share of their assets will go to their surviving children in equal proportions[‡]. In the absence of all of the above, the assets will go to _____.[§]

IN WITNESS WHEREOF I have hereunto set my hands on this _____ (DATE) at _____ (CITY).

SIGNATURE OF TESTATOR

SIGNED by the above-named testator as his/her last will and testament in our presence, who appear to have perfectly understood and approved the contents in the presence of both of us present, at the same time, who in his/her presence, and in the presence of each other, have hereunto subscribed our names as witnesses.

....

[†] Or whatever you want to give.
[‡] Or the proportions you specify.
[§] Decide where you want this to go.

WITNESSES

1. Name: _____

   Date: _____

   Place: _____

   PAN: _____

   Aadhaar: _____

   Contact details: _____

   Signature: _____

2. Name: _____

   Date: _____

   Place: _____

   PAN: _____

   Aadhaar: _____

   Contact details: _____

   Signature: _____

Author's Note

I know this was hard! But how do you feel after putting down all these details? I must tell you that once I finished this exercise, I felt really empowered. Not just as a gift to the family, but just for my own use, to have at hand all the details needed every once in a while is a big efficiency-enhancing exercise. The other thing that comes through sharply is the consolidation of the assets. Most households have, what I call, an asset bleed. There are assets created without a plan and the papers are scattered. This exercise is a great starting point to actually build a financial plan.

It is only when you sit down to consolidate your life as described by various financial and non-financial relationships that you realize how complicated our modern lives are. So many details, so much paperwork, so many relationships, so many usernames and passwords—it is almost a full-time job to keep it all afloat. I find that even with all my organizing skills, there are times that I feel things are out of control—a driving license not updated, an address change that is not reflecting—the list is endless.

I have found that order in the paperwork and order in the way files are stored on the computer are the foundation blocks of a more efficient life. How long should it take for you to send a soft copy of your Aadhaar to some agency? Not more than 20 seconds. How long should it take you to locate your class X marksheet? Not more than two minutes. How long to find your tax return filed ten years ago? Not more than two minutes. The more structure and order you build in this this part of your life; the more time is available to do the things you really like.

I have tried to think of as many details as possible but I am sure that there are plenty of things I might have left out. In fact, each time I discussed the book while it was being written, I got such great ideas for adding details. Please do reach out to me at mailme@monikahalan.com with your suggestions for the next edition of the book.

Ending with a quote of The Mother: 'To establish order around oneself helps to begin order within oneself.'

Acknowledgements

To The Mother and Sri Aurobindo for giving me the courage to talk about death fearlessly and honestly.

To Ananth Padmanabhan, CEO, HarperCollins India, who triggered the idea of a book with all the important details that make up our lives. This book is evidence that a casual conversation can turn into a book very quickly!

To Sachin Sharma, Associate Publisher, for the ideas that have taken the book forward and all the hard work behind the scenes. The long exchanges arguing over cover titles and design have been so worth it. Thank you for the suggestions on the preface and back cover of the book that have added so much value.

Thank you, Shreya Lall, for the edit and the suggestions. Much gratitude to Mukul Chand, the typesetter with HarperCollins India, who turned a difficult idea into reality. I'd like to thank Saurav Das for the cover design. I love the blue–gold colour play.

To R. Jagannathan, my first boss who remains a mentor and guide. Thank you for taking the time to read the manuscript and for adding the very thoughtful suggestions to the material in this book. I know you have been wanting me to do a much bigger book on estate planning. That is work in progress. Meanwhile, I hope this will be useful.

To Col Sanjeev Dwivedi, a reader of *Let's Talk Money*, who took the work forward by making a list of things that next of kin need to look out for. Thank you for sharing your work and I have certainly benefitted from it.

To my friends who have loved the idea of such a book and given thoughtful suggestions to make the book better. I must mention Gayatri Jayaraman, Deepti Bhaskaran, Kayezad E. Adajania and Vivina Vishwanathan who have been generous with their ideas for this book. I am grateful for the rich bouquet of advice that was given when I discussed my book with you.

To my daughter, Meera Chikermane, the brain scientist who keeps the encouragement going—you can do it mom!

To my husband, Gautam Chikermane, who sits with me and does the book editing so rigorously that I can only think back with sympathy about his team who must have suffered the same process.

To you, dear reader, for continuing to love my work. Thank you for reading. Now absorb and implement!

Finally, a quote of Sri Aurobindo:

Death is the mortal state of Matter with Mind and Life involved in it; Immortality is a state of infinite being, consciousness and bliss.

—*The Secret of the Veda*, p. 45

About the Author

Monika Halan's career spans across media, public policy and financial education. She is the founder of Dhan Chakra Financial Education and author of the bestselling book *Let's Talk Money* (HarperCollins, 2018) and *Let's Talk Mutual Funds* (HarperCollins, 2023). She has public policy experience and has served on several high-profile Government of India and SEBI committees. She has worked across various media organizations in India, including *Mint*, *The Economic Times* and *The Indian Express*, and was the editor of *Outlook Money*. She has run four successful TV series around personal finance on NDTV, Zee and Bloomberg India.

She has an MA in economics from the Delhi School of Economics and MA in journalism studies from the University of Wales. A Yale World Fellow (2011), Halan is based in New Delhi.

You can reach out to her at mailme@monikahalan.com

Also by Monika Halan

HarperCollins *Publishers* India

At HarperCollins India, we believe in telling the best stories and finding the widest readership for our books in every format possible. We started publishing in 1992; a great deal has changed since then, but what has remained constant is the passion with which our authors write their books, the love with which readers receive them, and the sheer joy and excitement that we as publishers feel in being a part of the publishing process.

Over the years, we've had the pleasure of publishing some of the finest writing from the subcontinent and around the world, including several award-winning titles and some of the biggest bestsellers in India's publishing history. But nothing has meant more to us than the fact that millions of people have read the books we published, and that somewhere, a book of ours might have made a difference.

As we look to the future, we go back to that one word—a word which has been a driving force for us all these years.

Read.